Belle's Christmas Surprise

CARRIE JOY SCHAFER KRAUSE

Belle's Christmas Surprise
Copyright © 2020 by Carrie Joy Schafer Krause

All rights reserved. No part of this publication may be reproduced, distributed, or transmitted in any form or by any means, including photocopying, recording, or other electronic or mechanical methods, without the prior written permission of the author, except in the case of brief quotations embodied in critical reviews and certain other non-commercial uses permitted by copyright law.

Tellwell Talent
www.tellwell.ca

ISBN
978-0-2288-3098-6 (Hardcover)
978-0-2288-3097-9 (Paperback)
978-0-2288-3099-3 (eBook)

For extra Christmas fun, search for a hidden candy cane on each of the Illustrator's pictures!

Special Thanks to:

- My amazing Mom, Alice Schafer, for always encouraging me to think, speak, write, teach, and love.
- My husband and best friend, Brent, for encouraging me to dream.

I love you truly.

- Artha Lee Gill, for sharing the information and pictures of your dear Mom.

Dedication

- To my beautiful Grandchildren: Andrew, Hayley, Kylee, Aiden, Hannah, Zachary, Caia, and those I haven't yet met. Always carry a pretty rock and a story in your pocket.

Belle lived with her family in a small cabin on the Canadian Prairie. Belle was born in 1912. Her father, Jessie, was a farmer. Her mother Bessie, looked after her family. Belle had eight brothers and sisters. She went to a school house on the prairie. All the children learned together in one big room. The older students helped the younger students. Belle knew it was a privilege to go to school.

The James children, Eda Belle is fourth from the right. Arlie is third from the right.

Joyful...... That was how Belle James felt that one Christmas many years ago.

It was Christmas Eve. Snowflakes slowly fell and covered an already full Winter ground of white. Soon her Father and the horses would be back from town. He had gone to get more hay. The animals would all get a little extra hay to eat---it was Christmas!

𝓑elle could hear the sound of bells ringing. She knew that sound. She had heard it many times before. It was the ringing and jingling of bells on the harnesses worn by the horses. Her Father was home from town. He had a fresh load of wonderful hay. This hay was the kind of hay a girl would lift to her nose to smell, jump in from the loft of the barn, and fork to feed the horses.

That night was a very special night, a night that Belle would never forget. Belle's Father brought hay for the horses and....

.....a very special Christmas gift for each of the children! This gift would be Belle's only Christmas gift.

Father asked each child to sit down, close their eyes, and hold out their hands.

Peeking was not allowed!

Belle waited patiently to feel the surprise in her hands. It was smooth. It felt sort of long and cold. The interesting thing was that Belle could smell a delicious scent coming from her gift in her hands. Belle wondered, "What could this be?"

Finally, Father gave the children permission to look.

Belle opened her eyes. It was a WIENER! It had been a very long time since Father had brought home this delicious treat. How wonderful! Belle truly felt like she was given a very special Christmas gift!

She held it in her hands. She smelled it. Every so often she would lick or nibble at her wiener. This truly was a very dear gift. Belle held the wiener gently, then she brought it up to her chest and held it close to her heart.

She never set it down once. She wanted it to last a long time, at least another day! Belle decided her treat was going to be saved so that she would have some for tomorrow, Christmas Day.

Soon it was bedtime. Belle jumped into bed between her two sisters. She drifted off to sleep that Christmas Eve, tucked inside her warm blankets holding her wiener between her hands and close to her heart.

The stars shone extra bright that Christmas Eve. Joy and love filled the crisp cold air. Hope for a wonderful Christmas Day was felt by a little prairie girl.

The early morning sun shone through the bedroom window. Christmas had arrived! Belle felt for her Christmas wiener. It wasn't there! She panicked! She sat up in her bed while searching in the blankets.

She began to cry. The tears trickled down her cheeks. Her wiener was so special to her! It was her only gift! What had happened? Where had it gone? Did someone do this? Belle sobbed. Her gift from her Father was missing.

Belle's sister, Arlie, and brother helped her look. The special Christmas gift could not be found.

Then their Mother made a discovery. She suggested that Belle go talk with Arlie.

Belle went to Arlie. The smell of a wiener could be found on her older sister's breath. Belle knew it was Arlie. Belle knew Arlie had been the one that had taken her wiener!

Throughout the day Belle thought of what her sister had taken from her. Belle felt angry at Arlie for taking something that didn't belong to her. Belle felt like she couldn't trust Arlie.

She felt sad. She would not get to enjoy her wiener this Christmas day. It was gone.

Later that afternoon, Arlie came to Belle and apologized. She was sorry. Belle accepted Arlie's apology. Arlie then gave Belle a frosted Syrup Cookie that she had saved from the treat bags given out at the church concert.

Joyful.....

Belle's smiles and forgiving spirit made Christmas Day wonderful! The neighbours came to share the day with the James family. The turkey dinner was delicious, especially with her Mom's Syrup Cookies for dessert.

The children played Fox and Geese out in the snow in the farmyard. The snow made great snow angels! Everyone went tobogganing down the coulee hill!

*B*ut, Belle had to say that the very best part of her Christmas was…….

.....eating half of her Christmas gift that year......

.........half of her wiener!

"Eda Belle is the second from the top with the bow in her hair."

"Eda Belle is the baby."

About the Real Belle

Eda Belle was born in 1912. She met and married a cowboy, named Arthur, in 1932. Eda Belle and Arthur were married for 77 years. She had a garden and was an amazing cook. She baked thousands of cinnamon buns and loaves of bread for the local market. Eda Belle learned how to play many instruments and loved to paint pictures. But the most amazing thing about Eda Belle was her friendliness and kindness she shared wherever she went. Eda Belle lived to be 99 years old.

"Eda Belle"

Extension Questions for Parents and Teachers

- √ Belle and her family were pioneers. What is a pioneer? (Noun)
- √ Pioneers are people who are living life in a new way. They are living using new ways to make life easier and better for themselves.
- √ To pioneer(verb) is to develop new ways of thinking and doing things.

? How was life different for Belle and her family living in 1912 on the Canadian prairie than it is for you?
? What is one difference that you wish we had now?
? What are some differences that you think made life more difficult?
? Why was it a surprise to you that Belle received a wiener for Christmas?
? How did you know Belle loved her gift?
? How would you feel if you received a wiener for a gift?
? Why did Belle hold the wiener close to her heart?
? What do you think are some lessons from this story?
? How could this story of Belle and her Christmas Surprise affect you and your life?
? What did you like least about this book?
? What other stories did this story remind you of?
? If you were making a movie of this book, who would you cast as Belle, or Arlie?
? What feelings did this book evoke for you?
? If you got the chance to ask the author of this book one question, what would it be?
? Which character in the book would you most like to meet?
? What do you think of the book's title? What other title might you choose?
? What do you think of the book's cover? How well does it convey what the book is about? Design your own cover for the story.
? What do you think the author's purpose was in writing this book? What ideas was she trying to convey?
? If you could hear this same story from another person's point of view, who would you choose?

Syrup Cookies

This is a cookie recipe that was often made at Christmas. The cookies were shared with friends and neighbors when they got together.

Arlie gave Belle her cookies that were found in the bag from the church Christmas Concert.

Makes a very large batch of cookies! Invite some friends to help make, and eat the cookies!

Preheat oven to 350 degrees F.

Mix the Ingredients below together until well mixed.

2 cups sugar
2 cups lard or shortening
1 cup syrup
1 cup of molasses
2 cup sour milk
4 eggs
3 teaspoons of baking soda
1 teaspoon ginger
Flour (12 cups or more!)

Cream the sugar and shortening together. Add the other ingredients except the flour. Once mixed, add enough flour so the dough can be rolled with a rolling pin.

Cut out cookie shapes using cookie cutters.

Bake for approximately 12-19 minutes until the cookies have risen and are slightly browned.

Cool.

These cookies can then be iced with your favorite icing recipe and decorated with sprinkles of all different shapes and colors!

"Syrup Cookies"

Walnut Christmas Tree Decorations

(Parent help needed!)

Making walnut tree decorations was an easy way for families to decorate their Christmas trees. A small note could be placed inside the nut when gluing it back together.

Walnuts
Thread or String (7-8 inches)
Glue or glue gun
Sharp knife – For parent use only!!

Preheat the over to 250 degrees F. Arrange the walnuts in a baking pan laying the nuts on the bottom of the pan. Bake for 35 minutes, then cool. Use a sharp knife to cut around the natural split in the shell. Clean the nut out of the inside. Take a seven-inch thread or string, fold in half and make a knot using the ends. Put the knotted end inside of the walnut. Glue the two sides of the walnut shell back together. Let the glue harden and place on your Christmas tree!

These are fancy walnuts, painted gold with ribbons!

www.ingramcontent.com/pod-product-compliance
Lightning Source LLC
LaVergne TN
LVHW070119080526
838200LV00080B/4697